KU-630-538

let's cook

low fat

Kathryn Hawkins

p

Contents

Winter Beef & Vegetable Soup

This comforting broth is perfect for a cold day and is sure to warm you up.

Serves 4

CALORIES PER SERVING: 161 • FAT CONTENT PER SERVING: 3.3 G

INGREDIENTS

60 g/2 oz/^{1}/$_3$ cup pearl barley
1.2 litres/2 pints/5 cups fresh beef
  stock
1 tsp dried mixed herbs
225 g/8 oz lean rump or sirloin beef

1 large carrot, diced
1 leek, shredded
1 medium onion, chopped
2 sticks celery, sliced
salt and pepper

2 tbsp fresh parsley, chopped,
  to garnish
crusty bread, to serve

1 Place the pearl barley in a large saucepan. Pour over the stock and add the mixed herbs. Bring to the boil, cover and simmer for 10 minutes.

2 Meanwhile, trim any fat from the beef and cut the meat into thin strips.

3 Skim away any scum that has risen to the top of the stock with a flat ladle.

4 Add the beef, carrot, leek, onion and celery to the pan.

Bring back to the boil, cover and simmer for about 20 minutes or until the meat and vegetables are just tender.

5 Skim away any remaining scum that has risen to the top of the soup with a flat ladle. Blot the surface with absorbent kitchen paper to remove any fat. Adjust the seasoning according to taste.

6 Ladle the soup into warm bowls and sprinkle with freshly chopped parsley. Serve accompanied with crusty bread.

VARIATION

This soup is just as delicious made with lean lamb or pork fillet. A vegetarian version can be made by omitting the beef and beef stock and using vegetable stock instead. Just before serving, stir in 175 g/ 6 oz fresh bean curd (tofu), drained and diced. An even more substantial soup can be made by adding other root vegetables, such as swede or turnip, instead of, or as well as, the carrot.

Tuscan Bean & Vegetable Soup

This thick, satisfying blend of beans and diced vegetables in a rich red wine and tomato stock, based on an Italian favourite, makes an ideal simple supper.

Serves 4

CALORIES PER SERVING: 156 • FAT CONTENT PER SERVING: 1.5 G

INGREDIENTS

1 medium onion, chopped
1 garlic clove, finely chopped
2 celery sticks, sliced
1 large carrot, diced
400 g/14 oz can chopped tomatoes
150 ml/5 fl oz/²/₃ cup Italian dry
   red wine

1.2 litres/2 pints/5 cups fresh
   vegetable stock
1 tsp dried oregano
425 g/15 oz can mixed beans
   and pulses
2 medium courgettes
   (zucchini), diced

1 tbsp tomato purée (paste)
salt and pepper

TO SERVE:
low-fat pesto sauce
crusty bread

1 Place the prepared onion, garlic, celery and carrot in a large saucepan. Stir in the tomatoes, red wine, vegetable stock and oregano.

2 Bring the vegetable mixture to the boil, cover and leave to simmer for 15 minutes. Stir the beans and courgettes (zucchini) into the mixture, and continue to cook, uncovered, for a further 5 minutes.

3 Add the tomato purée (paste) to the mixture and season well with salt and pepper to taste. Then heat through, stirring occasionally, for a further 2–3 minutes, but do not allow the mixture to boil again.

4 Ladle the soup into warm bowls and serve with a spoonful of low-fat pesto on each portion and accompanied with crusty bread.

VARIATION

For a more substantial soup, add 350 g/12 oz diced lean cooked chicken or turkey with the tomato purée (paste) in step 3.

Parsleyed Chicken & Ham Pâté

Pâté is easy to make at home, and this combination of lean chicken and ham mixed with herbs is especially straightforward.

Serves 4

CALORIES PER SERVING: 132 • FAT CONTENT PER SERVING: 1.8 G

INGREDIENTS

225 g/8 oz lean, skinless
  chicken, cooked
100 g/3^1/$_2$ oz lean ham, trimmed
small bunch fresh parsley
1 tsp lime rind, grated
2 tbsp lime juice

1 garlic clove, peeled
125 ml/4^1/$_2$ fl oz/^{1}/$_2$ cup low-fat
  natural fromage frais
  (unsweetened yogurt)
salt and pepper
1 tsp lime zest, to garnish

TO SERVE:
wedges of lime
crisp bread
green salad

1 Dice the chicken and ham and place in a blender or food processor. Add the parsley, lime rind and juice, and garlic and process well until finely minced. Alternatively, finely chop the chicken, ham, parsley and garlic and place in a bowl. Mix gently with the lime rind and juice.

2 Transfer the mixture to a bowl and mix in the fromage frais (yogurt). Season with salt and pepper to taste, cover and leave to chill in the refrigerator for about 30 minutes.

3 Pile the pâté into individual serving dishes and garnish with lime zest. Serve the pâtés with lime wedges, crisp bread and a fresh green salad.

VARIATION

This pâté can be made equally successfully with other kinds of minced, lean, cooked meat such as turkey, beef and pork. Alternatively, replace the chicken and ham with peeled prawns (shrimp) and/or white crab meat or with canned tuna in brine, drained. Remember that removing the skin from poultry reduces the fat content of any dish.

Pork Stroganoff

Tender, lean pork, cooked in a rich tomato sauce with mushrooms and a green (bell) pepper, is flavoured with the extra tang of natural (unsweetened) yogurt.

Serves 4

CALORIES PER SERVING: 197 • FAT CONTENT PER SERVING: 7 G

INGREDIENTS

350 g/12 oz lean pork fillet
1 tbsp vegetable oil
1 medium onion, chopped
2 garlic cloves, crushed
25 g/1 oz plain (all-purpose) flour
2 tbsp tomato purée (paste)

425 ml/15 fl oz/1³/4 cups fresh
 chicken or vegetable stock
125 g/4¹/2 oz button mushrooms,
 sliced
1 large green (bell) pepper, deseeded
 and diced
¹/2 tsp ground nutmeg

4 tbsp low-fat natural (unsweetened)
 yogurt, plus extra to serve
salt and pepper
white rice, freshly boiled, to serve
ground nutmeg, to garnish

1 Trim away any excess fat and silver skin from the pork, then cut the meat into slices 1 cm/¹/2 inch thick.

2 Heat the oil in a large saucepan and gently fry the pork, onion and garlic for 4–5 minutes until lightly browned.

3 Stir in the flour and tomato purée, pour in the stock and stir to mix thoroughly.

4 Add the mushrooms, (bell) pepper, seasoning and nutmeg. Bring to the boil, cover and simmer for 20 minutes until the pork is tender and cooked through.

5 Remove the saucepan from the heat and stir in the yogurt.

6 Serve the pork and sauce on a bed of rice with an extra spoonful of yogurt and garnish with a dusting of ground nutmeg.

COOK'S TIP

You can buy ready-made meat, vegetable and fish stocks from leading supermarkets. Although more expensive they are better nutritionally than stock cubes which are high in salt and artificial flavourings. Home-made stock is best of all.

Pork with Ratatouille Sauce

Serve this delicious combination of meat and vegetables
with baked potatoes for an appetizing supper dish.

Serves 4

CALORIES PER SERVING: 214 • FAT CONTENT PER SERVING: 5.6 G

INGREDIENTS

4 lean, boneless pork chops, about
   125 g/4^1/$_2$ oz each
1 tsp dried mixed herbs
salt and pepper
baked potatoes, to serve

SAUCE:
1 medium onion
1 garlic clove
1 small green (bell) pepper
1 small yellow (bell) pepper
1 medium courgette (zucchini)

100 g/3^1/$_2$ oz button mushrooms
400 g/14 oz can chopped tomatoes
2 tbsp tomato purée (paste)
1 tsp dried mixed herbs
1 tsp caster (superfine) sugar

1 To make the sauce, peel and chop the onion and garlic. Deseed and dice the (bell) peppers. Trim and dice the courgette (zucchini). Wipe and halve the mushrooms.

2 Place all of the vegetables in a saucepan and stir in the chopped tomatoes and tomato purée (paste). Add the dried herbs, sugar and plenty of seasoning. Bring to the boil, cover and simmer for 20 minutes.

3 Meanwhile, preheat the grill (broiler) to medium. Trim away any excess fat from the chops, then season on both sides and rub in the dried mixed herbs. Cook the chops for 5 minutes, then turn over and cook for a further 6–7 minutes until cooked through.

4 Drain the chops on absorbent kitchen paper and serve accompanied with the sauce and baked potatoes.

COOK'S TIP

This vegetable sauce could be served with any other grilled (broiled) or baked meat or fish. It would also make an excellent filling for Crêpes.

Pan-seared Beef with Ginger, Pineapple & Chilli

Serve these fruity, hot and spicy steaks with noodles. Use a non-stick, ridged
frying pan (skillet) for the best results – it will help you cook with a minimum of fat.

Serves 4

CALORIES PER SERVING: 191 • FAT CONTENT PER SERVING: 5.1 G

INGREDIENTS

4 lean beef steaks (such as rump,
   sirloin or fillet), 100 g/3¹/₂ oz each
2 tbsp ginger wine
2.5 cm/1 inch piece root (fresh)
   ginger, finely chopped
1 garlic clove, crushed (minced)
1 tsp ground chilli

1 tsp vegetable oil
red chilli strips, to garnish
salt and pepper

TO SERVE:
freshly cooked noodles
2 spring onions (scallions), shredded

RELISH:
225 g/8 oz fresh pineapple
1 small red (bell) pepper
1 red chilli
2 tbsp light soy sauce
1 piece stem ginger in syrup, drained
   and chopped

1 Trim any excess fat from the beef if necessary. Using a meat mallet or covered rolling pin, pound the steaks until 1 cm/¹/₂ inch thick. Season on both sides and place in a shallow dish.

2 Mix the ginger wine, root (fresh) ginger, garlic and chilli and pour over the meat. Cover and chill for 30 minutes.

3 Meanwhile, make the relish. Peel and finely chop the pineapple and place it in a bowl. Halve, deseed and finely chop the (bell) pepper and chilli. Stir into the pineapple together with the soy sauce and stem ginger. Cover and chill until required.

4 Brush a non-stick frying pan (skillet) with the oil and heat until very hot. Drain the beef and add to the pan, pressing down to seal. Lower the heat and cook for 5 minutes. Turn the steaks over and cook for a further 5 minutes.

5 Drain the steaks on kitchen paper and transfer to serving plates. Garnish with chilli strips, and serve with noodles, spring onions (scallions) and the relish.

Minty Lamb Burgers

A tasty alternative to traditional hamburgers, these lamb burgers are flavoured with mint and are accompanied with a smooth minty dressing.

Serves 4

CALORIES PER SERVING: 237 • FAT CONTENT PER SERVING: 7.8 G

INGREDIENTS

350 g/12 oz lean lamb, minced (ground)
1 medium onion, finely chopped
4 tbsp dry wholemeal breadcrumbs
2 tbsp mint jelly
salt and pepper

TO SERVE:
4 wholemeal baps, split
2 large tomatoes, sliced
small piece of cucumber, sliced
lettuce leaves

RELISH:
4 tbsp low-fat natural fromage frais (unsweetened yogurt)
1 tbsp mint jelly, softened
5 cm/2 inch piece of cucumber, finely diced
1 tbsp fresh mint, chopped

1 Place the lamb in a large bowl and mix in the onion, breadcrumbs and jelly. Season well, then mould the ingredients together with your hands to form a firm mixture.

2 Divide the mixture into 4 and shape each portion into a round measuring 10 cm/4 inches across. Place the rounds on a plate lined with baking parchment and leave to chill for 30 minutes.

3 Preheat the grill (broiler) to medium. Line a grill rack with baking parchment, securing the ends under the rack, and place the burgers on top. Cook for 8 minutes, then turn over the burgers and cook for a further 7 minutes or until cooked through.

4 Meanwhile, make the relish. Mix together the fromage frais (unsweetened yogurt), mint jelly, cucumber and freshly chopped mint in a bowl. Cover and leave to chill in the refrigerator until required.

5 Drain the burgers on absorbent kitchen paper. Serve the burgers inside the baps and top with sliced tomatoes, cucumber, lettuce and relish.

Tricolour Chicken & Spinach Lasagne

A delicious pasta bake that is filled with the colours of the Italian flag – red from the tomatoes, green from the spinach and pasta, and white from the chicken and the sauce.

Serves 4

CALORIES PER SERVING: 424 • FAT CONTENT PER SERVING: 7.2 G

INGREDIENTS

350 g/12 oz frozen chopped spinach, thawed and drained

1/2 tsp ground nutmeg

450 g/1 lb lean, cooked chicken meat, skinned and diced

4 sheets no-pre-cook lasagne verde

1 1/2 tbsp cornflour (cornstarch)

425 ml/15 fl oz/1 3/4 cups skimmed milk

4 tbsp Parmesan cheese, freshly grated

salt and pepper

freshly prepared salad, to serve

TOMATO SAUCE:

400 g/14 oz can chopped tomatoes

1 medium onion, finely chopped

1 garlic clove, crushed (minced)

150 ml/5 fl oz/2/3 cup white wine

3 tbsp tomato purée (paste)

1 tsp dried oregano

1 Preheat the oven to 200°C/400°F/Gas Mark 6. To make the tomato sauce, place the tomatoes in a saucepan and stir in the onion, garlic, wine, tomato purée (paste) and oregano. Bring to the boil and simmer for 20 minutes until thick. Season well.

2 Drain the spinach again and spread it out on absorbent kitchen paper to make sure that as much water as possible has been removed. Layer the spinach in the base of an ovenproof baking dish. Sprinkle with nutmeg and season.

3 Arrange the diced chicken over the spinach and spoon over the tomato sauce. Arrange the sheets of lasagne over the tomato sauce.

4 Blend the cornflour (cornstarch) with a little of the milk to make a paste. Pour the remaining milk into a saucepan and stir in the cornflour (cornstarch) paste. Heat for 2–3 minutes, stirring, until the sauce thickens. Season well.

5 Spoon the sauce over the lasagne and transfer the dish to a baking sheet. Sprinkle the grated cheese over the sauce and bake in the oven for 25 minutes until golden-brown. Serve with a fresh green salad.

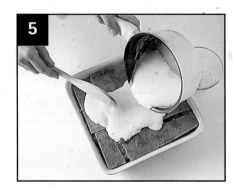

Lime Chicken Skewers with Mango Salsa

These succulent chicken kebabs (kabobs) are coated in a sweet lime dressing and are best served with a lime and mango relish. They make a refreshing light meal.

Serves 4

CALORIES PER SERVING: 200 • FAT CONTENT PER SERVING: 1.5 G

INGREDIENTS

4 boneless chicken breasts, skinned, about 125 g/4^1/$_2$ oz each
3 tbsp lime marmalade
1 tsp white wine vinegar
^{1}/$_2$ tsp lime rind, finely grated
1 tbsp lime juice

salt and pepper

TO SERVE:
lime wedges
boiled white rice, sprinkled with chilli powder

SALSA:
1 small mango
1 small red onion
1 tbsp lime juice
1 tbsp fresh coriander (cilantro), chopped

---

1 Slice the chicken breasts into thin pieces and thread on to 8 skewers so that the meat forms an S-shape down each skewer.

2 Preheat the grill (broiler) to medium. Arrange the chicken skewers on the grill (broiler) rack. Mix together the marmalade, vinegar, lime rind and juice. Season with salt and pepper to taste. Brush the dressing generously over the chicken and grill for 5 minutes. Turn the chicken over, brush with the dressing again and grill for a further 4–5 minutes until the chicken is cooked through.

3 Meanwhile, prepare the salsa. Peel the mango and slice the flesh off the smooth, central stone. Dice the flesh into small pieces and place in a small bowl.

4 Peel and finely chop the onion and mix into the mango, together with the lime juice and chopped coriander (cilantro). Season, cover and chill until required.

5 Serve the chicken kebabs (kabobs) with the salsa, accompanied with wedges of lime and boiled rice sprinkled with chilli powder.

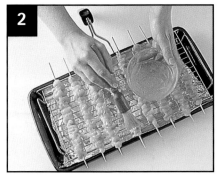

Crispy-Topped Stuffed Chicken

An attractive main course of chicken breasts filled with mixed (bell) peppers and set on a sea of red (bell) peppers and tomato sauce.

Serves 4

CALORIES PER SERVING: 211 • FAT CONTENT PER SERVING: 3.8 G

INGREDIENTS

4 boneless chicken breasts, about 150 g/5¹/₂ oz each, skinned
4 sprigs fresh tarragon
¹/₂ small orange (bell) pepper, deseeded and sliced
¹/₂ small green (bell) pepper, deseeded and sliced

15 g/¹/₂ oz wholemeal breadcrumbs
1 tbsp sesame seeds
4 tbsp lemon juice
1 small red (bell) pepper, halved and deseeded
200 g/7 oz can chopped tomatoes

1 small red chilli, deseeded and chopped
¹/₄ tsp celery salt
salt and pepper
fresh tarragon, to garnish

1 Preheat the oven to 200°C/ 400°F/Gas Mark 6. Slit the chicken breasts with a small, sharp knife to create a pocket in each. Season inside each pocket.

2 Place a sprig of tarragon and a few slices of orange and green (bell) peppers in each pocket. Place the chicken breasts on a non-stick baking sheet and sprinkle over the breadcrumbs and sesame seeds.

3 Spoon 1 tbsp lemon juice over each chicken breast and bake in the oven for 35–40 minutes until the chicken is tender and cooked through.

4 Meanwhile, preheat the grill (broiler) to hot. Arrange the red (bell) pepper halves, skin side up, on the rack and cook for 5–6 minutes until the skin blisters. Leave to cool for 10 minutes, then peel off the skins.

5 Put the red (bell) pepper in a blender, add the tomatoes, chilli and celery sal and process for a few seconds. Season to taste. Alternatively, finely chop the red (bell) pepper and rub through a sieve with the tomatoes and chilli.

6 When the chicken is cooked, heat the sauce, spoon a little on to a warm plate and arrange a chicken breast in the centre. Garnish with tarragon and serve.

Chicken with a Curried Yogurt Crust

A spicy, Indian-style coating is baked around lean chicken to give a full flavour.
Serve hot or cold with a tomato, cucumber and coriander (cilantro) relish.

Serves 4

CALORIES PER SERVING: 176 ● FAT CONTENT PER SERVING: 2 G

INGREDIENTS

1 garlic clove, crushed (minced)
2.5 cm/1 inch piece root (fresh)
  ginger, finely chopped
1 fresh green chilli, deseeded and
  finely chopped
6 tbsp low-fat natural (unsweetened)
  yogurt
1 tbsp tomato purée (paste)

1 tsp ground turmeric
1 tsp garam masala
1 tbsp lime juice
4 boneless, skinless chicken breasts,
  each 125 g/4^1/$_2$ oz
salt and pepper
wedges of lime or lemon, to serve

RELISH:
4 medium tomatoes
^{1}/$_4$ cucumber
1 small red onion
2 tbsp fresh coriander (cilantro),
  chopped

1 Preheat the oven to 190°C/
375°F/Gas Mark 5. In a small
bowl mix together the garlic,
ginger, chilli, yogurt, tomato
purée (paste), turmeric, garam
masala, lime juice and seasoning.

2 Wash and pat dry the chicken
breasts and place them on a
baking sheet. Brush or spread the
spicy yogurt mix over the chicken
and bake in the oven for 30–35

minutes until the meat is tender
and cooked through.

3 Meanwhile, make the relish.
Finely chop the tomatoes,
cucumber and onion and mix
together with the coriander
(cilantro). Season, cover and chill
until required.

4 Drain the cooked chicken on
absorbent kitchen paper and

serve hot with the relish. Or, allow
to cool, chill for at least 1 hour and
serve sliced as part of a salad.

VARIATION

*The spicy yogurt coating would
work just as well if spread on a
chunky white fish such as cod fillet.
The cooking time should be reduced
to 15–20 minutes.*

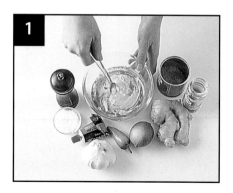

Fish Cakes with Piquant Tomato Sauce

*The combination of pink- and white-fleshed fish transforms
the humble fish cake into something a bit special.*

Serves 4

CALORIES PER SERVING: 320 • FAT CONTENT PER SERVING: 7.5 G

INGREDIENTS

450 g/1 lb potatoes, diced
225 g/8 oz haddock fillet
225 g/8 oz trout fillet
1 bay leaf
425 ml/15 fl oz/1³/4 cups fresh
   fish stock
2 tbsp low-fat natural fromage frais
   (unsweetened yogurt)

4 tbsp fresh snipped chives
75 g/2³/4 oz dry white breadcrumbs
1 tbsp sunflower oil
salt and pepper
fresh snipped chives, to garnish
lemon wedges, to serve

PIQUANT TOMATO SAUCE:
200 ml/7 fl oz/³/4 cup passata (sieved
   tomatoes)
4 tbsp dry white wine
4 tbsp low-fat natural (unsweetened)
   yogurt
chilli powder

1 Place the potatoes in a
saucepan and cover with
water. Bring to the boil and cook
for 10 minutes or until tender.
Drain well and mash.

2 Meanwhile, place the fish in a
pan with the bay leaf and
stock. Bring to the boil and
simmer for 7–8 minutes until
tender. Remove the fish with a
slotted spoon and flake the flesh
away from the skin.

3 Gently mix the cooked fish
with the potato, fromage frais
(unsweetened yogurt), chives and
seasoning. Leave to cool, then
cover and leave to chill for 1 hour.

4 Sprinkle the breadcrumbs on
to a plate. Divide the fish
mixture into 8 and form each
portion into a patty, about 7.5 cm/
3 inches in diameter. Press each
fish cake into the breadcrumbs,
coating all over.

5 Brush a frying pan (skillet)
with oil and fry the fish cakes
for 6 minutes. Turn the fish cakes
over and cook for a further 5–6
minutes until golden. Drain on
kitchen paper and keep warm.

6 To make the sauce, heat the
passata (sieved tomatoes) and
wine. Season, remove from the heat
and stir in the yogurt. Return to the
heat, sprinkle with chilli powder
and serve with the fish cakes.

Smoky Fish Pie

This flavoursome fish pie is perfect for a light supper.

Serves 4

CALORIES PER SERVING: 510 • FAT CONTENT PER SERVING: 6 G

INGREDIENTS

900 g/2 lb smoked haddock or
  cod fillets
600 ml/1 pint/2^1/$_2$ cups
  skimmed milk
2 bay leaves
115 g/4 oz button mushrooms,
  quartered

115 g/4 oz frozen peas
115 g/4 oz frozen sweetcorn kernels
675 g/1^1/$_2$ lb potatoes, diced
5 tbsp low-fat natural (unsweetened)
  yogurt
4 tbsp chopped fresh parsley

60 g/2 oz smoked salmon, sliced into
  thin strips
3 tbsp cornflour (cornstarch)
25 g/1 oz smoked cheese, grated
salt and pepper
wedges of lemon, to garnish

1 Preheat the oven to 200°C/
400°F/Gas Mark 6. Place the
fish in a pan and add the milk and
bay leaves. Bring to the boil, cover
and then simmer for 5 minutes.

2 Add the mushrooms, peas and
sweetcorn to the pan, bring
back to a simmer, cover and cook
for 5–7 minutes. Leave to cool.

3 Place the potatoes in a
saucepan, cover with water,
boil and cook for 8 minutes. Drain

well and mash with a fork or a
potato masher. Stir in the yogurt,
parsley and seasoning. Set aside.

4 Using a slotted spoon, remove
the fish from the pan. Flake
the cooked fish away from the skin
and place in an ovenproof gratin
dish. Reserve the cooking liquid.

5 Drain the vegetables,
reserving the cooking liquid,
and gently stir into the fish
together with the salmon strips.

6 Blend a little cooking liquid
into the cornflour (cornstarch)
to make a paste. Transfer the rest
of the liquid to a saucepan and add
the paste. Heat through, stirring,
until thickened. Discard the bay
leaves and season to taste.

7 Pour the sauce over the fish
and vegetables. Spoon over the
mashed potato so that the fish is
covered, sprinkle with cheese and
bake for 25–30 minutes. Garnish
with lemon wedges and serve.

Tuna Steaks with Fragrant Spices & Lime

Fresh tuna steaks are very meaty – they have a firm texture, yet the flesh is succulent. This recipe would be an impressive addition to a barbecue.

Serves 4

CALORIES PER SERVING: 200 • FAT CONTENT PER SERVING: 3.5 G

INGREDIENTS

4 tuna steaks, 175 g/6 oz each
1/2 tsp finely grated lime rind
1 garlic clove, crushed
2 tsp olive oil
1 tsp ground cumin

1 tsp ground coriander
pepper
1 tbsp lime juice
2 tbsp chopped fresh coriander
(cilantro)

TO SERVE:
avocado relish (see Cook's Tip,
below)
lime wedges

1 Trim the skin from the tuna steaks, rinse and pat dry on absorbent kitchen paper.

2 In a small bowl, mix together the lime rind, garlic, olive oil, cumin, coriander and pepper to make a paste.

3 Spread the paste thinly on both sides of the tuna. Heat a non-stick, ridged frying pan (skillet) until hot and press the tuna steaks into the pan to seal them. Lower the heat and cook for 5 minutes. Turn the fish over and cook for a further 4–5 minutes until the fish is cooked through. Drain on absorbent kitchen paper and transfer to a serving plate.

4 Sprinkle the lime juice and chopped coriander (cilantro) over the fish. Serve with freshly made avocado relish (see Cook's Tip, right) and lime wedges.

COOK'S TIP

For low-fat avocado relish to serve with tuna, peel and remove the stone from one small ripe avocado. Toss in 1 tbsp lime juice. Mix in 1 tbsp freshly chopped coriander (cilantro) and 1 small finely chopped red onion. Stir in some chopped fresh mango or a chopped medium tomato and season well.

Pesto Pasta

Italian pesto is usually laden with fat. This version has just as much flavour but is much healthier.

Serves 4

CALORIES PER SERVING: 350 • FAT CONTENT PER SERVING: 4.5 G

INGREDIENTS

225 g/8 oz chestnut mushrooms, sliced
150 ml/5 fl oz/³/₄ cup fresh vegetable stock
175 g/6 oz asparagus, trimmed and cut into 5 cm/2 inch lengths
300 g/10¹/₂ oz green and white tagliatelle

400 g/14 oz canned artichoke hearts, drained and halved
Grissini (bread sticks), to serve

TO GARNISH:
basil leaves, shredded
Parmesan shavings

PESTO:
2 large garlic cloves, crushed
15 g/¹/₂ oz fresh basil leaves, washed
6 tbsp low-fat natural fromage frais (unsweetened yogurt)
2 tbsp freshly grated Parmesan cheese
salt and pepper

1 Place the sliced mushrooms in a saucepan along with the stock. Bring to the boil, cover and simmer for 3–4 minutes until just tender. Drain and set aside, reserving the liquor to use in soups if wished.

2 Bring a small saucepan of water to the boil and cook the asparagus for 3–4 minutes until just tender. Drain and set aside until required.

3 Bring a large pan of lightly salted water to the boil and cook the tagliatelle according to the instructions on the packet. Drain, return to the pan and keep warm.

4 Meanwhile, make the pesto. Place all of the ingredients in a blender or food processor and process for a few seconds until smooth. Alternatively, finely chop the basil and mix all the ingredients together.

5 Add the mushrooms, asparagus and artichoke hearts to the pasta and cook, stirring, over a low heat for 2–3 minutes. Remove from the heat, mix with the pesto and transfer to a warm bowl. Garnish with shredded basil leaves and Parmesan shavings and serve with Grissini (bread sticks).

Char-grilled Mediterranean Vegetable Skewers

This medley of (bell) peppers, courgettes (zucchini), aubergine (eggplant) and red onion can be served on its own or as an unusual side dish.

Makes 8

CALORIES PER SERVING: 65 • FAT CONTENT PER SERVING: 2.5 G

INGREDIENTS

1 large red (bell) pepper	2 tbsp lemon juice	TO SERVE:
1 large green (bell) pepper	1 tbsp olive oil	cracked wheat
1 large orange (bell) pepper	1 garlic clove, crushed	tomato and olive relish
1 large courgette (zucchini)	1 tbsp chopped, fresh rosemary *or*	
4 baby aubergines (eggplant)	1 tsp dried	
2 medium red onions	salt and pepper	

1 Halve and deseed the (bell) peppers and cut into even sized pieces, about 2.5 cm/1 inch wide. Trim the courgettes (zucchini), cut in half lengthwise and slice into 2.5 cm/1 inch pieces. Place the (bell) peppers and courgettes (zucchini) into a large bowl and set aside.

2 Trim the aubergines (eggplant) and quarter them lengthwise. Peel the onions, then cut each one into 8 even-sized wedges. Add the aubergines annd onions to the bowl containing the (bell) peppers and courgettes (zucchini).

3 In a small bowl, mix together the lemon juice, olive oil, garlic, rosemary and seasoning. Pour the mixture over the vegetables and stir to coat.

4 Preheat the grill (broiler) to medium. Thread the vegetables on to 8 skewers. Arrange the skewers on the rack and cook for 10–12 minutes, turning frequently until the vegetables are lightly charred and just softened.

5 Drain the vegetable skewers and serve on a bed of cracked wheat accompanied with a tomato and olive relish, if wished.

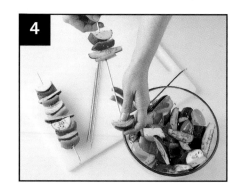

Mushroom Cannelloni

Thick pasta tubes are filled with a mixture of seasoned chopped mushrooms, and baked in a rich fragrant tomato sauce. Serve with shavings of Parmesan, if wished.

Serves 4

CALORIES PER SERVING: 315 • FAT CONTENT PER SERVING: 3.5 G

INGREDIENTS

350 g/12 oz chestnut mushrooms, chopped finely
1 medium onion, chopped finely
1 garlic clove, crushed
1 tbsp chopped fresh thyme
$^1/_2$ tsp ground nutmeg
4 tbsp dry white wine
4 tbsp fresh white breadcrumbs

12 dried 'quick-cook' cannelloni
salt and pepper
25 g/1 oz piece Parmesan cheese, to garnish (optional)

TOMATO SAUCE:
1 large red (bell) pepper
200 ml/7 fl oz/$^3/_4$ cup dry white wine
450 ml/16 fl oz/2 cups passata (sieved tomatoes)
2 tbsp tomato purée (paste)
2 bay leaves
1 tsp caster (superfine) sugar

1 Preheat the oven to 200°C/ 400°F/Gas Mark 6. Place the mushrooms, onion and garlic in a pan. Stir in the thyme, nutmeg and 4 tbsp wine. Bring to the boil, cover and simmer for 10 minutes.

2 Stir in the breadcrumbs to bind the mixtture together and season. Cool for 10 minutes.

3 Preheat the grill (broiler) to hot. To make the sauce, halve and deseed the (bell) pepper, place on the grill (broiler) rack and cook for 8–10 minutes until charred. Leave to cool for 10 minutes.

4 Once the (bell) pepper has cooled, peel off the charred skin. Chop the flesh and place in a food processor with the wine. Blend until smooth, and pour into a pan.

5 Mix the remaining sauce ingredients with the (bell) pepper and wine and season. Bring to the boil and simmer for 10 minutes. Discard the bay leaves.

6 Cover the base of an ovenproof dish with a thin layer of sauce. Fill the cannelloni with the mushroom mixture and place in the dish. Spoon over the remaining sauce, cover with foil and bake for 35–40 minutes. Garnish with Parmesan (if using) and serve.

Ratatouille Vegetable Grill

Ratatouille is a French classic – a sumptuous dish of vegetables cooked in a tomato and herb sauce. Here it has a topping of diced potatoes and a golden layer of cheese.

Serves 4

CALORIES PER SERVING: 330 • FAT CONTENT PER SERVING: 4 G

INGREDIENTS

2 medium onions
1 garlic clove
1 medium red (bell) pepper
1 medium green (bell) pepper
1 medium aubergine (eggplant)

2 medium courgettes (zucchini)
2 x 400 g/14 oz cans chopped
   tomatoes
1 bouquet garni
2 tbsp tomato purée (paste)

900 g/2 lb potatoes
75 g/2³/₄ oz reduced-fat Cheddar
   cheese, grated
salt and pepper
2 tbsp snipped fresh chives, to garnish

1 Peel and finely chop the onions and garlic. Rinse, deseed and slice the (bell) peppers. Rinse, trim and cut the aubergine (eggplant) into small dice. Rinse, trim and thinly slice the courgettes (zucchini).

2 Place the onion, garlic and (bell) peppers into a large saucepan. Add the tomatoes, and stir in the bouquet garni, tomato purée (paste) and salt and pepper to taste. Bring to the boil, cover and simmer for 10 minutes, stirring half-way through.

3 Stir in the prepared aubergine (eggplant) and courgettes (zucchini) and cook, uncovered, for a further 10 minutes, stirring occasionally.

4 Meanwhile, peel the potatoes and cut into 2.5 cm/1 inch cubes. Place the potatoes into another saucepan and cover with water. Bring to the boil and cook for 10–12 minutes until tender. Drain and set aside.

5 Transfer the vegetables to a heatproof gratin dish. Pile the cooked potato cubes evenly over the vegetables.

6 Preheat the grill (broiler) to medium. Sprinkle grated cheese over the potatoes and place under the grill for 5 minutes until golden, bubbling and hot. Serve garnished with snipped chives.

Chicken & Spinach Salad

A simple combination of lean chicken with fresh young spinach leaves and a few fresh raspberries is served with a refreshing yogurt and honey dressing. This recipe is perfect for a summer lunch.

Serves 4

CALORIES PER SERVING: 225 • FAT CONTENT PER SERVING: 6 G

INGREDIENTS

4 boneless, skinless chicken breasts, 150 g/5^1/$_2$ oz each
450 ml/16 fl oz/2 cups fresh chicken stock
1 bay leaf
225 g/8 oz fresh young spinach leaves

1 small red onion, shredded
115 g/4 oz fresh raspberries
salt and freshly ground pink peppercorns
fresh toasted croûtons, to garnish

DRESSING:
4 tbsp low-fat natural (unsweetened) yogurt
1 tbsp raspberry vinegar
2 tsp clear honey

1 Place the chicken breasts in a frying pan (skillet). Pour over the stock and add the bay leaf. Bring to the boil, cover and simmer for 15–20 minutes, turning half-way through, until the chicken is cooked through. Allow to cool in the liquid.

2 Arrange the spinach on 4 serving plates and top with the onion. Cover and leave to chill.

3 Drain the cooked chicken and pat dry on absorbent kitchen paper. Slice the chicken breasts thinly and arrange, fanned out, over the spinach and onion. Sprinkle with the raspberries.

4 To make the dressing, mix all the ingredients together in a small bowl. Drizzle a spoonful of dressing over each chicken breast and season with salt and ground

pink peppercorns to taste. Serve with freshly toasted croûtons.

VARIATION

This recipe is delicious with smoked chicken, but it will be more expensive and richer, so use slightly less. It would make an impressive starter for a dinner party.

Almond Trifles

Amaretti biscuits can be made with ground almonds, which give them a high fat content. For this recipe, make sure you use the biscuits made from apricot kernels, which have a lower fat content.

Serves 4

CALORIES PER SERVING: 230 • FAT CONTENT PER SERVING: 3.5 G

INGREDIENTS

8 Amaretti di Saronno biscuits
4 tbsp brandy *or* Amaretti liqueur
225 g/8 oz raspberries, thawed
   if frozen

300 ml/^{1}/$_2$ pint/1^1/$_4$ cups
   low-fat custard
300 ml/^{1}/$_2$ pint/1^1/$_4$ cups low-fat
   natural fromage frais
   (unsweetened yogurt)

1 tsp almond essence (extract)
15 g/^{1}/$_2$ oz toasted almonds,
   flaked (slivered)
1 tsp cocoa powder

1 Place the biscuits in a mixing bowl and using a rolling pin, carefully crush the biscuits into small pieces.

2 Divide the crushed biscuits among 4 serving glasses. Sprinkle over the brandy or liqueur and leave to stand for about 30 minutes to allow the biscuits to soften.

3 Top the layer of biscuits with a layer of raspberries, reserving a few raspberries for decoration, and spoon over enough custard to just cover.

4 Mix the fromage frais (unsweetened yogurt) with the almond essence (extract) and spoon over the custard. Leave to chill in the refrigerator for about 30 minutes.

5 Just before serving, sprinkle over the toasted almonds and dust with cocoa powder. Decorate with the reserved raspberries and serve at once.

VARIATION

Try this trifle with assorted summer fruits. If they are a frozen mix, use them frozen and allow them to thaw so that the juices soak into the biscuit base – it will taste delicious.

Tropical Fruit Fool

Fruit fools are always popular, and this lightly tangy version will be no exception. Use your favourite fruits in this recipe if you prefer.

Serves 4

CALORIES PER SERVING: 170 • FAT CONTENT PER SERVING: 0.6 G

INGREDIENTS

1 medium ripe mango
2 kiwi fruit
1 medium banana
2 tbsp lime juice

1/2 tsp finely grated lime rind, plus
  extra to decorate
2 medium egg whites
425 g/15 oz can low-fat custard

1/2 tsp vanilla essence (extract)
2 passion fruit

1 To peel the mango, slice either side of the smooth, flat central stone. Roughly chop the flesh and blend the fruit in a food processor or blender until smooth. Alternatively, mash with a fork.

2 Peel the kiwi fruit, chop the flesh into small pieces and place in a bowl. Peel and chop the banana and add to the bowl. Toss all of the fruit in the lime juice and rind and mix well.

3 In a grease-free bowl, whisk the egg whites until stiff and then gently fold in the custard and vanilla essence (extract) until thoroughly mixed.

4 In 4 tall glasses, alternately layer the chopped fruit, mango purée and custard mixture, finishing with the custard on top. Leave to chill in the refrigerator for 20 minutes.

5 Halve the passion fruits, scoop out the seeds and spoon the passion fruit over the fruit fools. Decorate each serving with the extra lime rind and serve.

VARIATION

Other tropical fruits to try include papaya purée, with chopped pineapple and dates, and tamarillo or pomegranate seeds to decorate. Or make a summer fruit fool by using strawberry purée, topped with raspberries and blackberries, with cherries to finish.

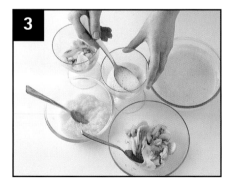

Baked Apples with Blackberries

*This winter dessert is a classic dish. Large, fluffy apples are hollowed out
and filled with spices, almonds and blackberries. Serve hot with low-fat custard.*

Serves 4

CALORIES PER SERVING: 250 • FAT CONTENT PER SERVING: 2 G

INGREDIENTS

4 medium-sized cooking apples
1 tbsp lemon juice
100 g/3^1/$_2$ oz prepared blackberries,
    thawed if frozen
15 g/^{1}/$_2$ oz flaked (slivered) almonds

^{1}/$_2$ tsp ground allspice
^{1}/$_2$ tsp finely grated lemon rind
2 tbsp demerara (brown crystal)
    sugar
300 ml/^{1}/$_2$ pint/1^1/$_4$ cups ruby port

1 cinnamon stick, broken
2 tsp cornflour (cornstarch) blended
    with 2 tbsp cold water
low-fat custard, to serve

1 Preheat the oven to 200°C/
400°F/Gas Mark 6. Wash and
dry the apples. Using a small
sharp knife, make a shallow cut
through the skin around the
middle of each apple – this will
help the apples to cook through.

2 Core the apples, brush the
centres with the lemon juice
to prevent browning and stand in
a shallow ovenproof dish.

3 In a bowl, mix together the
blackberries, almonds, allspice,
lemon rind and sugar. Using a
teaspoon, spoon the mixture into
the centre of each apple.

4 Pour the port into the tin, add
the cinnamon stick and bake
the apples in the oven for 35–40
minutes or until tender and soft.
Drain the cooking juices into a pan
and keep the apples warm.

5 Discard the cinnamon and
add the cornflour (cornstarch)
mixture to the cooking juices.
Heat, stirring, until thickened.

6 Heat the custard until piping
hot. Pour the sauce over the
apples and serve with the custard.

VARIATION

*Use raspberries
instead of blackberries and, if you
prefer, replace the port with
unsweetened orange juice.*

This is a Parragon Book
First published in 2003

Parragon
Queen Street House
4 Queen Street, Bath, BA1 1HE, UK

Copyright © Parragon 2003

All recipes and photography compiled from material cre-
ated by 'Haldane Mason', and 'The Foundry'.

Cover design by Shelley Doyle.

All rights reserved. No part of this publication may be
reproduced, stored in a retrieval system or transmitted,
in any form or by any means, electronic, mechanical,
photocopying, recording or otherwise, without the prior
permission of the copyright holder.

ISBN: 1-40540-826-X

Printed in China

NOTE

This book uses imperial and metric measurements. Follow the same
units of measurement throughout; do not mix imperial and metric. All
spoon measurements are level; teaspoons are assumed to be 5 ml and
tablespoons are assumed to be 15 ml. Unless otherwise stated, milk is
assumed to be whole milk, eggs and individual vegetables such as potatoes are medium, and pepper is freshly ground black pepper.

The times given for each recipe are an approximate guide only because
the preparation times may differ according to the techniques used by dif-
ferent people and the cooking times may vary as a result of the type of
oven used.

Recipes using raw or very lightly cooked eggs should be avoided by
infants, the elderly, pregnant women, convalescents and anyone suffer-
ing from an illness.